A Note from the Author

"To all the pizza enthusiasts, delivery aficionados, and curious minds,

This book is dedicated to the devoted individuals who strive to understand and optimise the art of pizza delivery. From the passionate pizzaiolos crafting the perfect pies to the logistics wizards orchestrating seamless deliveries, this dedication is a tribute to your commitment and ingenuity.

In exploring Pizza Delivery: A Kanban Story' we embark on a journey to unravel the intricate web of logistics, technology, and customer satisfaction that underpins the world of pizza delivery. Through this dedication, we celebrate the relentless pursuit of excellence and the tireless dedication to mastering the nuances of order tracking in the realm of pizza.

May this book serve as an illuminating guide for all those who seek to elevate the pizza delivery experience, harness the power of efficient processes, and embrace the symbiotic relationship between order tracking and the principles of Kanban. Here's to unlocking new possibilities, fostering innovation, and delighting pizza lovers around the world.

Introduction

In the fast-paced world of pizza delivery, efficiency, accuracy, and customer satisfaction are paramount. Pizza restaurants have embraced the power of technology to enhance the ordering experience, and one of the notable advancements is the implementation of online order tracking systems. These systems allow customers to monitor the progress of their pizza orders, from the moment they are placed to the moment they arrive at their doorstep.

By providing real-time updates and status notifications, online order tracking systems have revolutionised the way customers interact with and anticipate their pizza deliveries. In this book, we will delve into the science behind this concept, exploring the activities that occur at each status update, the benefits of the process, and how it relates to the Kanban methodology. Join us as we unravel the inner workings of the pizza order tracking system and discover how it has transformed the pizza delivery experience for both customers and pizza restaurants alike.

The Author

Julian Cambridge was born in London, UK.

- M.Sc. Business Computing
- B.Sc. (Hons) Computing with Business

Julian founded Golden Agile Solutions to supply IT consultancy activities to clients.

- Accredited Kanban Trainer (AKT, KMP, TKP)
- Certified Scrum Professional (CSM, CSPO, A-CSM, A-CSPO, CSP-SM)
- ICAgile Authorized Instructor (Agile Fundamentals, Agile Product Ownership, Agile Testing, Business Agility)

Online Order Tracking System

An online order tracking system is a technological solution implemented by businesses to allow customers to monitor the progress of their orders in real-time. It provides visibility into the various stages of order processing, from placement to fulfilment, and sometimes even delivery.

The key components of an online order tracking system typically include:

1. Order Placement: Customers can place their orders through a website, mobile app, or other online platforms. They provide necessary details such as item selections, quantities, delivery address, and payment information.

2. Order Confirmation: After the order is placed, customers receive an order confirmation that verifies the details of their purchase. This confirmation serves as a reference point for tracking the order's progress.

3. Order Processing: Once the order is confirmed, it enters the processing phase. This involves activities such as inventory management, order assembly, and scheduling for fulfilment.

4. Status Updates: Throughout the order processing journey, customers receive status updates at different stages. These updates inform customers about the progress of their orders, such as order received, preparation, cooking, quality check, packaging, and dispatch.

5. Real-Time Tracking: Many online order tracking systems provide real-time tracking capabilities. Customers can access a tracking link or enter their order number on a tracking page to view the live status of their order. This feature often includes estimated delivery times and, in some cases, the ability to track the delivery driver's location.

6. Notifications: Customers may receive notifications via email, SMS, or push notifications to keep them informed about any changes in the order status or estimated delivery time.

The benefits of an online order tracking system are numerous:

1. Enhanced Customer Experience: Real-time tracking provides customers with a sense of control and transparency. They can anticipate the arrival of their orders and plan accordingly, reducing uncertainty and improving overall satisfaction.

2. Efficiency and Accuracy: The system streamlines order processing, minimising errors and delays. It improves communication between different teams involved in order fulfilment, such as kitchen staff, delivery drivers, and customer service.

3. Operational Insights: The data collected through the online order tracking system can provide valuable insights into order volumes, peak hours, popular items, and customer preferences. This information can help businesses optimise their operations and make data-driven decisions.

4. Customer Support: If customers have any questions or concerns about their orders, the online tracking system provides an opportunity for them to contact customer support directly and receive prompt assistance.

Overall, an online order tracking system is a valuable tool that enhances the customer experience, improves operational efficiency, and supports effective communication between businesses and their customers.

Tracking Process
for Pizza Delivery

The concept of tracking pizza orders online involves a combination of technology, logistics, and customer service to provide real-time updates on the progress of your order. Let's break down each status and the activities associated with them:

1. Order: This status indicates that your order has been received and entered into the system. At this stage, the restaurant begins processing your request and preparing the necessary ingredients.

2. Prep: Once your order is in the preparation phase, the pizza makers start assembling the pizza according to your specifications. They will stretch the dough, add the sauce, cheese, and toppings, and prepare it for baking.

3. Baking: In this stage, the pizza is placed in the oven to cook at the appropriate temperature for a specific duration. The baking time may vary based on the type and size of the pizza.

4. Quality Check: After the pizza is baked, it undergoes a quality check to ensure that it meets the restaurant's standards. This step involves inspecting the pizza for

proper cooking, toppings distribution, and overall presentation.

5. Out for Delivery: Once the pizza passes the quality check, it is prepared for delivery. The restaurant notifies a delivery driver to pick up the order and delivers it to your specified address. During this stage, you can track the location of the delivery driver in real-time.

The benefits of this tracking process are numerous:

1. Transparency: The real-time updates provide transparency to customers, allowing them to monitor the progress of their order and estimate the delivery time. It enhances the overall customer experience by reducing uncertainty.

2. Customer Satisfaction: By providing status updates, the pizza chain demonstrates its commitment to customer service. It helps manage expectations and provides reassurance to customers that their order is being prepared and delivered promptly.

3. Efficiency: The tracking process enables better coordination between different stages of the pizza-making process. It helps streamline operations, reduce bottlenecks, and ensure timely delivery.

If these status updates were not in place, the process would lack transparency, and customers would be left in the dark about the progress of their order. They wouldn't know if their order had been received, if it was being prepared, or when it would be delivered. This could lead to frustration, uncertainty, and a diminished customer experience.

Kanban

In relation to Kanban, the tracking process shares some similarities. Kanban is a method used to manage and visualise workflow, typically represented by a Kanban board. Each status update in the pizza tracking process can be seen as a Kanban column representing a particular stage in the workflow.

As the order progresses from one stage to another, it moves across the Kanban board, providing visibility into the overall flow of orders. This helps identify potential bottlenecks, manage resources effectively, and maintain a smooth and efficient workflow.

The limitation of work in progress is evident as each order moves through distinct stages, ensuring that resources are allocated appropriately.

Case Studies

There are numerous case studies of pizza restaurants successfully implementing online order tracking systems. Here are a few examples:

1. Domino's Pizza: Domino's Pizza is a prominent example of a pizza chain that has effectively utilised online order tracking. They were one of the first chains to introduce a comprehensive tracking system called the "Domino's Tracker." Customers can place orders online and track their pizzas from the moment they are ordered until they are out for delivery. The Domino's Tracker provides real-time updates on the status of the order, including order confirmation, preparation, baking, quality check, and delivery. This system has contributed to Domino's reputation for transparency and customer service.

2. Pizza Hut: Pizza Hut is another major pizza chain that has implemented online order tracking. Their system allows customers to track their orders through the Pizza Hut app or website. The tracking process includes status updates such as order received, preparation, baking, quality check, and delivery. Customers can view the progress of their order in real-time and receive estimated delivery times. Pizza Hut's online order tracking system has been well-received by customers and has contributed to a positive user experience.

3. Papa John's: Papa John's, a global pizza chain, also offers an online order tracking system. Through their website or mobile app, customers can track their orders as they move through the various stages of preparation, baking, and delivery. Real-time updates are provided, giving customers visibility into the progress of their order. Papa John's online order tracking system has been praised for its accuracy and efficiency.

Furthermore, Papa John's has utilised the order tracking system to refine its kitchen operations. By analysing the time taken in each production stage, the company has implemented process improvements to ensure consistent order preparation times and minimise delays. This proactive approach has had a direct impact on customer satisfaction and order fulfilment speed.

4. Local Pizzeria: Local Pizzeria Case Study
Even smaller, independent pizzerias have recognised the value of order tracking systems. A local pizzeria, Stefano's Pizzeria, implemented a simple yet effective order tracking system that provides customers with updates on their orders via SMS and email. This system has proven instrumental in reducing customer anxiety, improving communication, and fostering a sense of trust and reliability.

Stefano's Pizzeria has leveraged data generated from the order tracking system to gain insights into peak ordering times, enabling better resource allocation and staffing optimisation. Through this data-driven approach, the pizzeria has been able to enhance its operational efficiency and customer service levels, leading to increased customer retention and positive word-of-mouth referrals.

These case studies demonstrate how pizza chains have successfully incorporated online order tracking systems into their operations. These systems have improved customer satisfaction, increased transparency, and provided a seamless ordering experience. By leveraging technology and effective communication, these pizza restaurants have enhanced their overall service and built customer loyalty.

Industry Challenges and Technical Considerations

While the online order tracking system implemented by pizza restaurants is generally reliable and beneficial, there have been a few instances where it has faced challenges or failed to meet customer expectations. Here are a couple of examples:

1. Technical Glitches: Like any technological system, online order tracking systems can experience technical glitches or malfunctions. In some cases, customers have reported issues such as inaccurate status updates, delays in updates, or complete system outages. These failures can lead to confusion and frustration among customers who rely on accurate tracking information.

2. Inadequate Staffing or Preparation: The online tracking system relies on efficient coordination between different stages of the pizza-making process. If a restaurant is understaffed or unprepared to handle a high volume of orders, it can result in delays and inconsistencies in the tracking system. For example, if the restaurant is overwhelmed with orders during peak hours, it may struggle to update the status of each order in a timely manner, leading to inaccurate or delayed tracking information.

3. Delivery Challenges: The tracking system primarily focuses on the progress of the order within the restaurant. However, once the pizza is out for delivery, external factors such as traffic congestion, weather conditions, or unforeseen circumstances can impact the delivery time. While these factors are beyond the control of the restaurant, customers may perceive the tracking system as a failure if their delivery is significantly delayed despite the status showing "out for delivery."

4. User Error or Miscommunication: Occasionally, issues with the tracking system can be attributed to user error or miscommunication. For example, if a customer enters an incorrect phone number or address during the order placement, it can lead to inaccurate tracking updates or failed deliveries. Similarly, if there is a miscommunication between the restaurant and the delivery driver, it can result in delays or confusion in the tracking system.

It's important to note that these instances of failure are relatively uncommon, and many pizza restaurants have implemented robust systems to minimise such issues. Additionally, when failures occur, reputable pizza chains typically take steps to address the problems, improve their systems, and provide compensation or alternative solutions to affected customers.

Life before Online Ordering Tracking Systems

Before the advent of online order tracking systems, the process of ordering and tracking deliveries was significantly different. Here's a glimpse into what life was like before the introduction of these systems:

1. Phone Orders: Customers would typically place their orders by calling the pizza restaurant directly. They would provide their order details, delivery address, and payment information over the phone. However, once the order was placed, there was limited visibility into its progress until the delivery arrived.

2. Uncertain Delivery Times: Without online tracking, customers had to rely on estimated delivery times provided by the restaurant at the time of ordering. These estimates were often approximate and could vary depending on factors such as order volume, traffic conditions, or the availability of delivery drivers.

3. Lack of Transparency: Customers had little to no visibility into the stages of order processing. They were unaware of when their order was being prepared, when it was out for delivery, or if there were any delays along

the way. This lack of transparency could lead to frustration and uncertainty.

4. Limited Communication: If customers had any questions or concerns about their orders, they typically had to call the restaurant and speak to a customer service representative. This process could be time-consuming and sometimes resulted in long wait times or miscommunication.

5. Reliance on Delivery Drivers: Customers heavily relied on the delivery drivers for updates regarding the progress of their orders. However, drivers were often busy and unable to provide real-time information, leaving customers in the dark about the whereabouts of their deliveries.

6. Inconvenience and Missed Expectations: Without online order tracking, customers had to be available at the delivery address during the estimated delivery window. If the delivery was delayed or arrived earlier than expected, it could result in missed deliveries or inconvenience for customers who were not prepared.

Overall, the absence of online order tracking systems meant that customers had limited visibility and control over their orders. The process relied heavily on phone communication and trust in the restaurant's ability to deliver within the estimated time frame. The introduction of online order tracking systems has transformed the customer experience by providing transparency, real-time updates, and a greater sense of control over the delivery process.

The future of Online Order Tracking Systems

The future of online order tracking systems is expected to see further advancements and innovations that will enhance the customer experience and streamline order fulfilment processes. Here are some potential trends and developments that may shape the future of these systems:

1. Integration of Advanced Technologies: Online order tracking systems may integrate emerging technologies such as artificial intelligence (AI) and machine learning (ML) to provide more accurate predictions and personalised experiences. AI-powered algorithms can analyse data from previous orders to estimate preparation and delivery times more accurately, taking into account factors like traffic, weather conditions, and historical order patterns.

2. Enhanced Delivery Tracking: Delivery tracking may become even more precise and detailed. GPS tracking technology can be utilised to provide customers with real-time updates on the exact location of their delivery driver. This level of granularity can help customers plan

their time better and reduce anxiety about the delivery's progress.

3. Integration with Smart Devices: As smart home devices gain popularity, online order tracking systems may integrate with these devices. Customers will be able to track their orders and receive updates through voice-activated assistants or smart displays, providing a seamless and hands-free tracking experience.

4. Augmented Reality (AR) Experiences: AR technology may be used to provide customers with interactive and immersive order tracking experiences. For example, customers could use their smartphones or AR-enabled glasses to visualise the progress of their order through virtual representations or animations.

5. Integration with Messaging Apps and Chatbots: Online order tracking systems may integrate with popular messaging apps to provide customers with status updates and allow them to communicate with customer support through chatbots. This integration can provide a more convenient and seamless tracking experience, allowing customers to receive updates and resolve issues directly within their preferred messaging app.

6. Sustainability and Eco-Friendly Practices: The future of online order tracking systems may also involve a focus on sustainability. Restaurants may implement eco-

friendly packaging and delivery practices and incorporate tracking updates related to sustainability initiatives, such as carbon footprint reduction or information about locally sourced ingredients.

Overall, the future of online order tracking systems will likely revolve around leveraging advanced technologies, improving accuracy and personalisation, and providing seamless integration with emerging platforms and devices. These advancements will contribute to a more convenient and satisfying customer experience while optimising operational efficiency for businesses in the food delivery industry.

Summary

The implementation of online order tracking systems in pizza restaurants has brought about significant improvements in customer satisfaction and operational efficiency. These systems allow customers to track the progress of their pizza orders in real-time, from the moment the order is received to its delivery.

Each status update, such as order, prep, baking, quality check, and out for delivery, represents a specific stage in the pizza-making process. The benefits of online order tracking include increased transparency, improved customer experience, and streamlined operations.

Without this system in place, customers would lack visibility into the progress of their orders, leading to frustration and uncertainty. The tracking process in pizza restaurants relates to the Kanban methodology, as it visualises the workflow and helps identify potential bottlenecks.

While there have been instances where the system has faced challenges or failed, overall, it has revolutionised the pizza delivery experience and become an essential tool for both customers and pizza restaurants.

Foundations of Scrum Agile
Education

£2.99

App Store

Google Play

Pizza Delivery: A Kanban Story.   24

www.ingramcontent.com/pod-product-compliance
Lightning Source LLC
La Vergne TN
LVHW051651050326
832903LV00034B/4821